TOMATOES

TOMATOES

southwater

This edition published by Southwater

Distributed in the UK by
The Manning Partnership
Batheaston, Bath BA1 7RL, UK
tel. (0044) 01225 852 727
fax. (0044) 01225 852 852

Distributed in the USA by
Ottenheimer Publishing
5 Park Center Court
Suite 300
Owing Mills MD 2117-5001, USA
tel. (001) 410 902 9100
fax. (001) 410 902 7210

Distributed in Australia by
Sandstone Publishing
56 John Street, Leichhardt
New South Wales 2040, Australia
tel. (0061) 2 9552 3815
fax. (0061) 2 9552 1538

Distributed in New Zealand by
Five Mile Press NZ
Unit 3/46a Taharoto Road, PO Box 33-1071
Takapuna, Auckland 9, New Zealand
tel. (0064) 9 486 1925
fax. (0064) 9 486 1454

Southwater is an imprint of
Anness Publishing Limited
© 1998, 2000 Anness Publishing Limited
1 3 5 7 9 10 8 6 4 2

Publisher: Joanna Lorenz
Senior Cookery Editor: Linda Fraser
Project Editor: Margaret Malone
Designer: Bill Mason
Illustrations: Anna Koska

Photographers: William Adams-Lingwood, Edward Allwright, David Armstrong, Steve Baxter, James Duncan,
Michelle Garrett, Amanda Heywood, David Jordan and Don Last
Recipes: Angela Boggiano, Carla Capalbo, Jacqueline Clark, Frances Cleary, Carole Clements, Joanna Farrow,
Christine France, Shirley Gill, Carole Handslip, Ruby Le Bois, Norma Miller, Janice Murfitt, Stuart Walton, Laura
Washburn, Kate Whiteman, Elizabeth Wolf-Cohen and Jeni Wright
Food for photography: Carole Handslip, Jane Hartshorn, Lucie McKelvie, Jane Stevenson, Judy Williams and
Elizabeth Wolf-Cohen
Stylists: Diana Civil, Maria Kelly, Blake Minton and Marian Price

Previously published as *Tomatoes: A Book of Recipes*
Printed and bound in Singapore

For all recipes, quantities are given in both metric and imperial measures and,
where appropriate, measures are also given in standard cups and spoons.
Follow one set, but not a mixture, because they are not interchangeable.

Contents

$\mathcal{I}$NTRODUCTION

Tomatoes are assuredly among every keen cook's favourite ingredients. Whether fresh, canned, bottled or sun-dried, they are always essential, adding their sweet distinctive flavour to salads, soups, sauces and a huge range of delicious vegetable, meat and pasta dishes.

Although eaten as a savoury food, tomatoes are in fact a fruit. Related to potatoes, aubergines and sweet peppers, the tomato plant also belongs to the same family that contains deadly nightshade, which explains why tomatoes were treated with such suspicion when they first arrived in Europe. These tomatoes were yellow and quickly earned the name 'love apples', perhaps because it was believed that the so-called poison acted as an aphrodisiac.

In England the plants were grown for decoration in gardens and even in Spain and Italy the fruit was only slowly accepted. The red tomato was not introduced to Europe until the eighteenth century, and only since then have tomatoes enjoyed their huge popularity. In Mediterranean countries today, tomatoes, along with garlic and olive oil, form the basis of so many meals that it's hard to find any recipes in which they don't appear.

There are countless varieties of tomato. Along with a great number of the familiar red salad varieties, there are yellow, orange and green tomatoes, as well as tomatoes that are striped, multicoloured and even variegated. They range in size from tiny cherry tomatoes to huge fruits that can weigh more than 500g/1¼lb each. The fuller-flavoured tomatoes tend to thrive in hotter places like southern Europe and California. However, tomatoes are grown successfully in almost all countries where there is some sunshine during the summer, and they are a huge favourite among gardeners due to their fuller flavour compared to the shop-bought variety.

The problem for shops and supermarkets is simply one of transit. In order that they are not over-ripe when they reach the shops, tomatoes have to be picked before they are quite ready. By the time they are on sale, tomatoes are (or at least should be) a beautiful glossy red. However, because they have ripened in transit, and not in sunshine, they are sadly less sweet and less full-flavoured. Only when you've sampled a sun-ripened tomato, picked fresh from the vine, do you really appreciate the difference.

You really can't go wrong with tomatoes, be they raw in a salad or as the basis for a rich sauce. The recipes in this book demonstrate just why the humble tomato is such an indispensable ingredient in any kitchen.

Types of Tomatoes

BEEFSTEAK TOMATOES

These are large pumpkin-shaped tomatoes. They have a good firm texture and a sweet, mellow flavour owing to their low acidity and are best eaten raw in salads and sandwiches. 'Brandywine' is considered one of the best-flavoured beefsteak tomatoes.

ROUND OR SALAD TOMATOES

There is a huge variety of salad tomatoes grown today, although most supermarkets offer a fairly limited selection. The red tomatoes, with their greater acidity and full flavour, are excellent whether for cooking or eating raw. Those with the best flavour, which are therefore the best choice for salads, have been sun-ripened, but if you don't have access to your own home-grown supply or a local farm shop, buy tomatoes on the vine, which also have an excellent flavour. For soups and sauces, buy soft, ripe fruit which has a fuller flavour.

YELLOW TOMATOES

'Yellow Canary' and 'Yellow Pear' are among the better known yellow tomatoes. They have a sweet, mild flavour, with lower acidity than red tomatoes, and are best used in salads or pickles.

ORANGE TOMATOES

Mild-flavoured tomatoes, with a sweet, delicate flavour and low acidity. Use in salads or for cold soups and sauces.

GREEN TOMATOES

Green, unripened tomatoes have traditionally been used for relishes and chutneys for hundreds of years. There are also tomatoes that are green when ripe. 'Green Grape', a variety of cherry tomato, has a green/yellow skin and a bright green flesh and is quite delicious in salads.

CHERRY TOMATOES

These small and dainty tomatoes are wonderfully sweet and are an excellent choice in salads or for cooking whole. There are varieties of cherry tomatoes in reds, yellows and oranges.

PLUM TOMATOES

These are richly flavoured with fewer seeds than round tomatoes. They are considered best in cooking, owing to their high acidity and concentrated flavour. Like cherry tomatoes, plum tomatoes are available in all sizes and colours; reds, however, are best for soups and sauces.

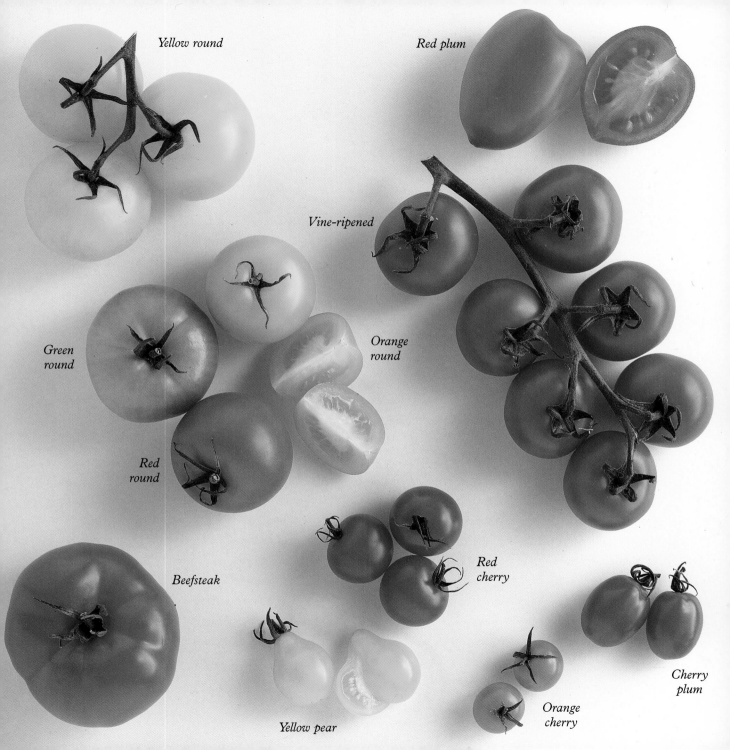

Yellow round

Red plum

Vine-ripened

Green round

Orange round

Red round

Beefsteak

Red cherry

Yellow pear

Orange cherry

Cherry plum

PROCESSED TOMATOES

SUN-DRIED TOMATOES

Sun-dried tomatoes are available loose or sold in olive oil in jars. They have a delicious, intense flavour and are used in cooking and in salads. Soak loose tomatoes in boiling water for about 15 minutes and then drain. Those in jars will keep for up to 1 year; use the oil in salad dressings.

SUN-DRIED TOMATO PURÉE

Use in sauces, soups and dips when you want a sun-dried tomato flavour. Since the tomatoes are preserved in oil, the purée is fairly rich and you may wish to reduce the amount of oil used in the recipe.

CANNED TOMATOES

Tomatoes are one of the few fruits that can be canned really successfully. They are excellent in tomato sauces for pastas and pizzas, having an intense and distinct flavour. Plum tomatoes are normally selected for canning and can be whole or chopped. Avoid those flavoured with herbs or garlic. It's simplicity itself to add your own flavour and you'll find it much more agreeable.

SUGOCASA

For special occasions, try sugocasa instead of ordinary canned tomatoes. Available in jars, the chopped plum tomatoes are mixed with tomato purée, giving the tomatoes a richer, fuller flavour. Ideal for pizza bases, sauces and stews.

PASSATA

Sometimes called creamed tomatoes, passata is made from canned tomatoes that have been puréed and sieved to remove the skin and seeds. A useful store-cupboard ingredient, it is invaluable in recipes like soups where you want a smooth result.

TOMATO PURÉE

Tomato purée is available in cans (where it is sometimes called paste) or in tubes. It adds a strong tomato flavour and bright colour to sauces and soups. Use sparingly, as the flavour is very intense and will overwhelm other ingredients given half the chance. Once opened, tomato purée should be stored in the fridge. Tubes of purée can be kept for up to 6 months. Canned purée will keep no more than 1 week.

Sun-dried
tomato purée

Chopped canned
tomatoes

Tomato purée

Canned plum tomatoes

Passata

Sun-dried tomatoes

Sugocasa

$\mathscr{B}$ASIC $\mathscr{T}$ECHNIQUES

COOKING WITH TOMATOES

PEELING TOMATOES

Cut a small cross in the skin at the base of each tomato and then plunge into boiling water. Leave for about 30 seconds or until the skin begins to roll back (it will depend on the type and ripeness of the tomato). Lift out with a slotted spoon, plunge briefly into cold water so that it is cool enough to handle and peel away the skin immediately. If the tomatoes are for a salad or to be eaten raw, plunge them into cold water for about 10 seconds before peeling away the skin, to prevent them softening any further.

SEEDING TOMATOES

Cut out the core from the top of the tomato and discard. Cut the tomato in half and gently squeeze each half, shaking the seeds and juice into a bowl. Scrape out any remaining seeds with a spoon or knife. If you are making a tomato sauce, you may like to place the seeds in a fine sieve and press them to extract more juice, which can then be added to the sauce.

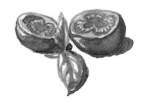

BASIC TOMATO SAUCE

This Italian tomato sauce is a useful standby for all sorts of dishes. When tomatoes are in season, make a large batch and freeze what you don't need to use immediately. Melt 25g/1oz butter in a saucepan and add 900g/2lb peeled, seeded and chopped tomatoes. Stir well, then cover and cook for 5 minutes. Add a good pinch of sugar and simmer, partly covered, for 30 minutes until the tomatoes have softened and the sauce is thick. Season to taste with salt and pepper. Makes 600ml/1 pint/2½ cups.

COOK'S TIPS

• *Selecting:* Choose red, ripe fruit, with leafy, green tops. Tomatoes sold on the vine have a fuller, sweeter flavour than loose tomatoes; better still are sun-ripened tomatoes.

• *Storing:* Keep tomatoes in a cool, dark place such as the salad drawer of the fridge, but allow them to come up to room temperature before eating. Paler tomatoes will redden if kept in a brown paper bag or in the salad drawer of the fridge.

• *Freezing:* Whole tomatoes tend to develop a mushy texture if frozen and thawed. It's better to peel, seed and roughly chop tomatoes and then freeze. Thoroughly defrost, then simply add to a recipe.

• *Roasting:* Tomatoes are superb roasted. Halve or chop tomatoes and place in a roasting tin. Add salt and olive oil. Roast in the oven at 220°C/425°F/Gas 7 for 25 minutes if chopped, a little longer if only halved.

BOTTLED CHERRY TOMATOES

These pretty cherry tomatoes, bottled with garlic and basil, are the perfect accompaniment to thick slices of country ham.

Prick 1kg/2¼lb cherry tomatoes with a toothpick and pack into clean, dry jars to within 2cm/¾in of the top, adding 5ml/1 tsp salt and 5ml/1 tsp sugar per 1 litre/1¾ pint/4 cup jar. Add fresh basil leaves and about 5 garlic cloves per jar. Rest the lids on the jars, but do not seal, and then stand on a baking sheet lined with a layer of cardboard. Bake in an oven at 120°C/250°F/Gas ½ for 45 minutes, until the juices simmer. Remove from the oven and seal the jars. Label and store in a cool place. Makes 1kg/2¼lb.

Soups and Starters

Whether for fresh summer gazpacho or creamy winter soups, tomatoes are everyone's favourite soup ingredient. For snacks and starters too, tomatoes come tops, adding their fresh flavour and wonderful colour to all sorts of dishes.

FRESH TOMATO SOUP

Naturally sweet, sun-ripened tomatoes are the best choice for this delicious soup.

Serves 6

1.5kg/3–3½ lb ripe tomatoes

400ml/14fl oz/1⅔ cups chicken or
vegetable stock

45ml/3 tbsp sun-dried tomato purée

30–45ml/2–3 tbsp balsamic vinegar

10–15ml/2–3 tsp caster sugar

small handful of basil leaves

salt and freshly ground black pepper

basil leaves, to garnish

toasted cheese croûtes and crème
fraîche, to serve

COOK'S TIP

The amount of caster sugar and
balsamic vinegar you need will
depend on the sweetness of the
tomatoes. Add a little to start
with, taste the soup and then
add more if necessary.

Peel the tomatoes by plunging them into boiling water for 30–40 seconds. Refresh in cold water and then peel away the skins. Cut them into quarters, discard the cores and place in a large saucepan. Add the chicken or vegetable stock and heat until just boiling. Reduce the heat, cover and simmer gently for 10 minutes until the tomatoes are pulpy.

Stir in the tomato purée, vinegar, sugar and basil. Season and cook gently for about 2 minutes, stirring occasionally. Pour the soup into a blender or food processor and blend until smooth. Reheat gently and serve with cheese croûtes and a little crème fraîche, garnished with basil.

GAZPACHO

Tomatoes and peppers are the essential ingredients in this classic Spanish soup. It is popular all over Spain, but nowhere more so than in Andalusia where there are hundreds of variations.

Serves 4

1.5kg/3–3½ lb ripe tomatoes

1 green pepper, seeded and roughly
*   chopped*

2 garlic cloves, crushed

2 slices white bread, crusts removed

60ml/4 tbsp olive oil

60ml/4 tbsp tarragon wine vinegar

150ml/¼ pint/⅔ cup tomato juice

good pinch of sugar

salt and freshly ground black pepper

For the garnishes

30ml/2 tbsp sunflower oil

2–3 slices white bread, diced

1 small cucumber, peeled and
*   finely diced*

1 small onion, finely chopped

1 red pepper, seeded and finely diced

1 green pepper, seeded and finely
*   diced*

2 hard-boiled eggs, chopped

Peel the tomatoes by plunging them into boiling water for 30–40 seconds. Refresh in cold water and then peel away the skins. Cut them into quarters and remove the cores. Place the green pepper in a blender or food processor and blend for a few seconds. Add the tomatoes, garlic, bread, olive oil and vinegar and process again. Add the tomato juice, sugar, seasoning and a little extra tomato juice or cold water and blend to mix. The soup should be fairly thick, but not stodgy. Pour the soup into a large bowl and chill for at least 2 hours but for no more than 12 hours.

Make the garnishes. Heat the sunflower oil in a frying pan and fry the bread cubes over a moderate heat for 4–5 minutes until golden brown. Drain well on kitchen paper. Place the croûtons together with the cucumber, onion, peppers and hard-boiled eggs in separate small dishes or, alternatively, arrange them in rows on a large plate.

Just before serving, stir a few ice cubes into the soup and then spoon into serving bowls. Serve with the garnishes.

TOMATO AND BLUE CHEESE SOUP

This unusual rich soup comes from the Northwest of America. It is a wonderful blend of flavours, the sweet, sharp quality of the tomatoes harmonizing with the strong and savoury taste of the cheese.

Serves 4

1.5kg/3–3½ lb ripe tomatoes

2 garlic cloves, very finely chopped

175g/6oz streaky bacon

30ml/2 tbsp sunflower oil or
 25g/1oz/2 tbsp butter

1 leek, finely chopped

1 carrot, finely chopped

1.2 litres/2 pints/5 cups unsalted
 chicken stock

115g/4oz/1 cup blue cheese,
 crumbled

45ml/3 tbsp whipping cream

a few fresh basil leaves or 1–2 fresh
 parsley sprigs

salt and freshly ground black pepper

COOK'S TIP
The rich, complex flavour and dry, crumbly texture of English Stilton make it a perfect choice for this dish.

Preheat the oven to 200°C/400°F/Gas 6. Peel the tomatoes by plunging them into boiling water for 30–40 seconds, refresh in cold water and then peel away the skins. Cut into quarters and discard the cores and seeds. Place in a shallow ovenproof glass or earthenware dish and sprinkle with the garlic and a little seasoning. Cook in the oven for 35 minutes. Grill or fry the bacon, cool and then crumble or finely chop. Set aside.

Heat the oil or butter in a large saucepan. Add the leek and carrot and a little seasoning and fry very gently for 10–12 minutes until softened, stirring occasionally. Stir in the stock and tomatoes, bring to the boil and then reduce the heat, cover and simmer for 20 minutes.

Add the blue cheese, cream and basil or parsley, reserving a few leaves to use as a garnish. Pour into a blender or food processor and blend until smooth. Pour the soup back into a clean pan and adjust the seasoning. Reheat without boiling and then ladle into warmed serving bowls. Sprinkle with the crumbed bacon, garnish with the reserved herbs and serve.

TOMATO AND GARLIC BREAD

The combination of tomatoes and garlic gives a wonderful Mediterranean flavour to bread. Serve with soup or with antipasti or tapas for a perfect snack or light meal.

Serves 4–6

4 large ripe tomatoes, roughly chopped
2 garlic cloves, roughly chopped
1.5ml/¼ tsp sea salt
grated rind and juice of ½ lemon
5ml/1 tsp soft light brown sugar
1 flat loaf of bread, such as ciabatta
30ml/2 tbsp olive oil
freshly ground black pepper

COOK'S TIP

This is a simple, rustic-style recipe and it's not necessary to peel the tomatoes. However, if you prefer a smoother paste, peel them before cooking.

Preheat the oven to 200°C/400°F/Gas 6. Place the tomatoes, garlic, salt, lemon rind and sugar in a small pan, cover and cook for 5 minutes until the tomatoes have released their juices and the mixture is quite watery.

Split the loaf in half horizontally and then cut each half widthways into two or three pieces. Place on a baking sheet and bake for 5–8 minutes until hot, crisp and golden brown.

While the bread is baking, add the lemon juice and olive oil to the tomatoes and cook, uncovered, for about 8 minutes until the mixture is thick and pulpy, stirring occasionally. Spread over the hot bread, sprinkle with pepper and serve.

TOMATOES WITH GUACAMOLE

Cherry tomatoes are just the right size for an easy nibble. For a special occasion, buy a selection of yellow and red tomatoes for a simple and colourful display.

Makes 24

24 cherry tomatoes

1 large ripe avocado, halved and
    stone removed

50g/2oz/¼ cup cream cheese

grated rind and juice of ½ lime

3–4 dashes Tabasco sauce

15–30ml/1–2 tbsp chopped fresh
    coriander

salt and freshly ground black pepper

sprigs of fresh coriander, to garnish

COOK'S TIP
The filling can be as mild or as spicy as you like. Add the Tabasco sauce to taste, mixing well after each addition.

Cut a slice from the bottom of each tomato and, using the handle of a small spoon, scoop out and discard the seeds. Sprinkle the tomato cavities with salt, then turn them over and drain on kitchen paper for about 30 minutes.

Scoop the flesh of the avocado into a food processor and add the cream cheese. Process until smooth. Add the lime rind and juice and the Tabasco sauce and season. Add half the chopped coriander and process to blend.

Spoon the mixture into a piping bag fitted with a medium star nozzle and pipe swirls into the tomatoes. Sprinkle with the remaining chopped coriander and arrange on a large serving plate. Garnish with coriander sprigs.

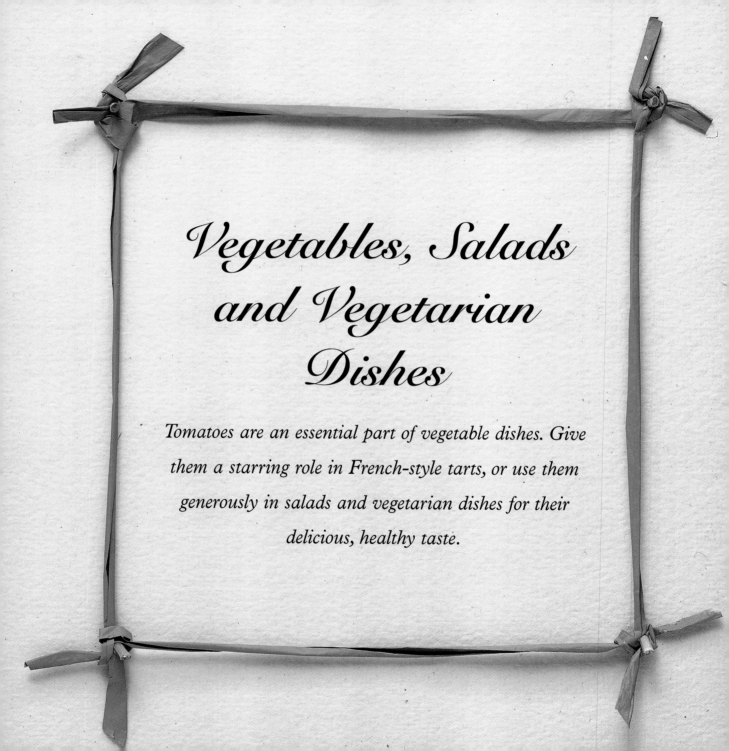

Vegetables, Salads and Vegetarian Dishes

Tomatoes are an essential part of vegetable dishes. Give them a starring role in French-style tarts, or use them generously in salads and vegetarian dishes for their delicious, healthy taste.

Sun-dried Tomatoes with Onions

Rich sun-dried tomatoes with rosemary and olive oil is a popular Tuscan combination and is a fine complement to sweet and tender baby onions.

Serves 4

450g/1lb button onions

10ml/2 tsp chopped fresh or
    1.5ml/¼ tsp dried rosemary

2 garlic cloves, chopped

15ml/1 tbsp chopped fresh parsley

50g/2oz/½ cup drained sun-dried
    tomatoes in oil, chopped

90ml/6 tbsp olive oil

15ml/1 tbsp white wine vinegar

salt and freshly ground black pepper

sprigs of fresh rosemary, to garnish

Preheat the oven to 150°C/300°F/Gas 2 and grease a shallow ovenproof baking dish. Cook the onions in boiling water for 5 minutes, drain and then spread over the bottom of the prepared dish. Mix together the rosemary, garlic, parsley and seasoning and sprinkle over the onions. Scatter the tomatoes over the top and drizzle with the olive oil and vinegar. Cover with a sheet of foil and bake in the oven for 45 minutes, basting occasionally.

Remove the foil, baste again with the liquid in the dish and cook for a further 15 minutes until the onions are completely tender and golden brown. Garnish with rosemary sprigs before serving.

TOMATO AND BASIL TART

This is a very simple yet extremely tasty tart, partnering tomatoes with mozzarella cheese and basil.

Serves 4

150g/5oz young mozzarella cheese,
   thinly sliced
4 large tomatoes, thickly sliced
about 10 basil leaves
30ml/2 tbsp olive oil
2 garlic cloves, thinly sliced
salt and freshly ground black pepper

For the pastry

115g/4oz/1 cup plain flour
50g/2oz/4 tbsp butter or margarine
1 egg yolk

Make the pastry. Mix the flour and a little salt, then rub in the butter or margarine and egg yolk. Add cold water to make a smooth dough and knead lightly. Chill for 1 hour. Preheat the oven to 190°C/375°F/Gas 5.

Remove the pastry from the fridge and allow 10 minutes for it to return to room temperature. Roll out into a 20cm/8in circle and press into the bottom of a 20cm/8in flan dish or tin. Prick all over with a fork and then bake in the oven for about 10 minutes until firm but not brown. Allow to cool slightly and reduce the oven temperature to 180°C/350°F/Gas 4.

Arrange the mozzarella slices over the pastry base and then place the tomatoes slices on top, overlapping slightly, but still in a single layer. Dip the basil leaves in olive oil and arrange them on the tomatoes. Scatter the garlic on top, drizzle with the remaining olive oil and season. Bake in the oven for 40–45 minutes until the tomatoes are well cooked. Serve hot.

TOMATO RISOTTO

Choose plump plum tomatoes for this dish for their fresh, vibrant flavour and firm texture.

Serves 4

675g/1½ lb firm ripe tomatoes,
  preferably plum
50g/2oz/4 tbsp butter
1 onion, finely chopped
275g/10oz/1½ cups Arborio rice
about 1.2 litres/2 pints/5 cups boiling
  vegetable stock
400g/14oz can cannellini beans,
  drained
50g/2oz/⅔ cup Parmesan cheese,
  grated
salt and freshly ground black pepper
10–12 basil leaves, shredded, and
  shavings of Parmesan cheese,
  to serve

Peel the tomatoes, cut in half and scoop out the seeds. Place the seeds in a sieve and press to extract the juice. Finely chop the tomato flesh. Melt the butter in a large pan and fry the onion for about 5 minutes until softened. Add the tomatoes, their juice and seasoning and cook for about 10 minutes, stirring occasionally. Add the rice, stir well and then add a ladleful of hot stock. Stir the mixture until the stock has been absorbed and continue adding and stirring in the stock until all the stock has been absorbed and the rice is tender.

Stir in the cannellini beans and Parmesan cheese and heat through for a few minutes. Just before serving, sprinkle each portion with shredded basil leaves and shavings of Parmesan cheese.

TOMATO AND COURGETTE BAKE

This popular French vegetable recipe is normally cooked in a tian *– a heavy earthenware dish.*
The tomatoes and courgettes are combined with rice, Parmesan cheese and fresh herbs.

Serves 4

45ml/3 tbsp olive oil

1 onion, chopped

1 garlic clove, crushed

3 lean bacon rashers, chopped

4 courgettes, grated

2 tomatoes, peeled, seeded and chopped

115g/4oz/1 cup cooked long-grain
  rice

10ml/2 tsp chopped fresh thyme

15ml/1 tbsp chopped fresh parsley

25g/1oz/4 tbsp grated Parmesan
  cheese

2 eggs, lightly beaten

15ml/1 tbsp fromage frais

salt and freshly ground black pepper

COOK'S TIP

For a dinner party, divide the
mixture among lightly greased
individual gratin dishes and
bake for 25 minutes until golden.

Preheat the oven to 180°C/350°F/Gas 4 and grease a shallow ovenproof dish with a little olive oil. Heat the rest of the oil in a large frying pan and fry the onion and garlic for about 5 minutes until softened. Add the bacon, fry for 2 minutes, and then stir in the courgettes and fry gently for a further 8 minutes, stirring occasionally and letting some of the liquid evaporate. Remove from the heat.

Add the tomatoes, rice, herbs, 30ml/2 tbsp of the Parmesan cheese, the eggs and fromage frais. Season with salt and pepper and stir well to mix. Spoon the mixture into the prepared dish and sprinkle over the remaining Parmesan cheese. Bake for 45 minutes until the mixture has set and is golden. Serve hot.

STUFFED TOMATOES WITH WILD RICE

These tomatoes are filled with a tasty wild rice mixture that could be served as a light meal with crusty bread and a salad, or as an accompaniment to grilled meat or fish.

Serves 4

8 medium tomatoes

50g/2oz/1/3 cup sweetcorn

30ml/2 tbsp white wine

50g/2oz/1/4 cup cooked wild rice

1 garlic clove, crushed

50g/2oz/1/2 cup Cheddar cheese, grated

15ml/1 tbsp chopped fresh coriander

15ml/1 tbsp olive oil

salt and freshly ground black pepper

Cut a slice off the tops of the tomatoes and scoop out the seeds with a small teaspoon. Discard the seeds and then scoop out the flesh. Chop the flesh and tops finely. Preheat the oven to 180°C/350°F/Gas 4 and lightly oil a shallow ovenproof dish.

Put the chopped tomatoes, sweetcorn and white wine in a saucepan, cover tightly and simmer for 4–5 minutes until the vegetables are tender. Drain off any excess liquid and then stir the wild rice, garlic, grated cheese, coriander and seasoning into the tomato mixture. Pile into the tomato shells and place these in the prepared dish. Sprinkle the tops with olive oil and bake in the oven for 15–20 minutes until cooked through.

COOK'S TIP
Either canned or frozen sweetcorn can be used for this dish. Fresh sweetcorn should be pre-cooked for 4–5 minutes until tender.

TOMATO AND MOZZARELLA SALAD

In this popular Italian salad the three principal ingredients represent the colours of the national flag. The natural acidity of the tomatoes means there is no need for vinegar or lemon juice in the dressing.

Serves 4

4 beefsteak tomatoes

400g/14oz mozzarella cheese

8–10 fresh basil leaves

60ml/4 tbsp olive oil

salt and freshly ground black pepper

COOK'S TIP
In Italy, the most sought-after mozzarella is made from the milk of water buffalo. It is found mainly in the south of Italy and in Campania.

Slice the tomatoes and mozzarella into thick rounds and arrange these overlapping on a serving dish, interspersed with basil leaves. Sprinkle with olive oil and a little salt and serve with black pepper which is normally passed round separately.

TOMATO AND FETA CHEESE SALAD

Sweet, sun-ripened tomatoes are rarely more delicious than when served with feta cheese and olive oil. This salad, popular in Greece and Turkey, is enjoyed as a light meal with warm bread.

Serves 4

900g/2lb tomatoes

200g/7oz feta cheese

120ml/4fl oz/½ cup olive oil, preferably Greek

12 black olives

freshly ground black pepper

Slice the tomatoes thickly and arrange them in a shallow serving dish. Crumble the cheese over the tomato slices and sprinkle with the olive oil. Scatter the olives over the top and season with black pepper. Serve at room temperature.

COOK'S TIP

Feta cheese has a strong salty flavour. The least salty varieties are imported from Greece and Turkey. If these are not available, rinse the feta in cold water to remove any brine before crumbling it over the salad.

Meat, Poultry and Fish

Tomatoes are one of our most versatile foods and
whether cooked in a sauce for chicken or fish, or
combined with meat, they magically bring
flavours together for some of our
best-loved dishes.

MEATBALLS IN TOMATO SAUCE

In this popular tapas dish, the meatballs are cooked in a tomato sauce that is sharpened with wine and flavoured with rosemary. The combination of the two is superb.

Serves 4

225g/8oz minced lamb or beef

4 spring onions, thinly sliced

2 garlic cloves, finely chopped

30ml/2 tbsp freshly grated Parmesan
 cheese

10ml/2 tsp fresh thyme leaves

15ml/1 tbsp olive oil

3 tomatoes, chopped

30ml/2 tbsp red or dry white wine

10ml/2 tsp chopped fresh rosemary

pinch of sugar

salt and freshly ground black pepper

fresh thyme, to garnish

COOK'S TIP

Although traditionally a tapas dish, this could be served with pasta or warm crusty bread as a meal for two.

Place the minced meat in a bowl and add the spring onions, garlic, Parmesan cheese, thyme and plenty of salt and pepper. Mix until thoroughly blended and then shape the mixture into 12 small firm balls.

Heat the oil in a large frying pan and cook the meatballs for about 5 minutes until evenly browned, turning frequently. Add the chopped tomatoes, wine, rosemary and sugar and season with salt and pepper. Cover and cook gently for 15 minutes until the tomatoes are soft and the meatballs are cooked through. Serve hot, garnished with thyme.

OSSO BUCO

This famous dish is made with osso buco – slices of veal knuckle – from which the dish gets its name.
Italian housewives would use their own bottled plum tomatoes, but canned tomatoes work equally well.

Serves 4

30ml/2 tbsp plain flour

4 pieces of osso buco (about
   1kg/2¼ lb veal knuckle, cut into
   4 slices, each about 2.5cm/1in
   thick, enclosing a piece of bone)

2 small onions

30ml/2 tbsp olive oil

1 celery stick, finely chopped

1 carrot, finely chopped

2 garlic cloves, finely chopped

400g/14oz can chopped tomatoes

300ml/½ pint/1¼ cups dry white wine

300ml/½ pint/1¼ cups chicken or
   veal stock

1 strip thinly pared lemon rind

2 bay leaves, plus extra to garnish

salt and freshly ground black pepper

green salad, to serve

For the gremolata

30ml/2 tbsp chopped fresh parsley

finely grated rind of 1 lemon

1 garlic clove, finely chopped

Preheat the oven to 160°C/325°F/Gas 3. Put the flour and a little seasoning in a large plastic bag and add the veal pieces, one by one, shaking the bag in order to coat them with flour. Shake off the excess flour. Slice one of the onions into rings. Heat the oil in a large flameproof casserole and add the veal and onion rings. Brown the meat on both sides and transfer to a plate. Chop the remaining onion and add to the pan with the celery, carrot and garlic, stirring well to incorporate all the pan juices and sediment. Cook gently for about 5 minutes until the vegetables are slightly softened, stirring frequently.

Add the chopped tomatoes, wine, stock, lemon rind and bay leaves and season well with salt and pepper. Bring to the boil, stirring, and then add the veal, turning to coat in the sauce. Cover and cook in the oven for 2 hours until the meat is tender.

Meanwhile, make the gremolata. Mix together the chopped parsley, grated lemon rind and garlic.

When the meat is tender, remove and discard the strip of lemon rind and bay leaves from the casserole and adjust the seasoning. Spoon the osso buco on to serving plates and sprinkle with the gremolata. Garnish with extra bay leaves, if liked, and serve with a green salad.

BEEF STEW WITH TOMATOES

This Italian dish is a rich stew of beef combined with creamed tomatoes and tomato purée. Cook it until it is melt-in-the-mouth tender; the perfect dish for a winter evening.

Serves 4

30ml/2 tbsp plain flour
10ml/2 tsp chopped fresh or
  5ml/1 tsp dried thyme
900g/2lb braising or stewing steak,
  cut into large cubes
45ml/3 tbsp olive oil
1 onion, roughly chopped
450ml/³/4 pint/1³/4 cups passata
250ml/8fl oz/1 cup beef stock
250ml/8fl oz/1 cup red wine
2 garlic cloves, crushed
30ml/2 tbsp tomato purée
225g/8oz/2 cups shelled fresh peas
5ml/1 tsp sugar
salt and freshly ground black pepper
fresh thyme sprigs, to garnish
new potatoes, to serve

Preheat the oven to 160°C/325°F/Gas 3. Put the flour, thyme and a little seasoning in a large plastic bag and add the cubes of beef, shaking the bag in order to coat the meat evenly with flour. Shake off the excess flour.

Heat the oil in a large flameproof casserole and brown the beef on all sides. Transfer to a plate with a slotted spoon. Add the onion to the pan and cook gently for 3 minutes until softened, stirring frequently. Stir in the passata, stock, wine, garlic and tomato purée and bring to the boil, stirring all the time. Add the beef, stir well to coat with the sauce and then cover and cook in the oven for 1¹/₂ hours.

When the meat is nearly tender, stir in the peas and sugar, return the casserole to the oven and cook for a further 30 minutes until the beef is very tender. Taste and adjust the seasoning. Serve with new potatoes, garnished with sprigs of fresh thyme.

CHICKEN WITH CAJUN SAUCE

Cayenne pepper gives heat to this tasty sauce of tomatoes, green pepper, celery and onions.

Serves 4

1 chicken, about 1.5kg/3–3½ lb
90g/3½ oz/¾ cup plain flour
250ml/8fl oz/1 cup buttermilk or milk
salt and freshly ground black pepper
vegetable oil, for frying
fresh parsley sprigs, to garnish

For the sauce

115g/4oz lard or vegetable fat
65g/2½ oz/½ cup plain flour
2 onions, chopped
2–3 celery sticks, chopped
1 large green pepper, seeded and
  chopped
2 garlic cloves, finely chopped
250ml/8fl oz/1 cup passata
450ml/¾ pint/1¾ cups red wine or
  chicken stock
225g/8oz tomatoes, peeled, seeded
  and chopped
2 bay leaves
15ml/1 tbsp soft brown sugar
5ml/1 tsp grated orange rind
2.5ml/½ tsp cayenne pepper

Make the sauce. Melt the lard or vegetable fat in a large heavy pan and stir in the flour. Cook over a moderately low heat, stirring constantly, for 15–20 minutes until the mixture is a deep hazelnut brown. Add the onions, celery, green pepper and garlic and continue cooking for 5–6 minutes until the vegetables have softened, stirring occasionally. Add the passata, wine or chicken stock, tomatoes, bay leaves, sugar, orange rind and cayenne pepper and season with salt. Bring to the boil and then simmer for 1 hour until the sauce is rich and thick, stirring from time to time.

While the sauce is cooking, cut the chicken into 8 pieces. Put the flour in a plastic bag with some salt and pepper. Dip each piece of chicken in buttermilk or milk and then dredge in the flour to coat lightly and evenly, shaking off any excess flour. Set the chicken aside for 20 minutes for the coating to set before frying.

Heat about 2.5cm/1in of oil in a large frying pan until very hot and beginning to sizzle. Fry the chicken pieces for about 30 minutes until cooked through and a deep golden brown. Drain the chicken on kitchen paper and then add to the sauce. Stir to coat thoroughly in the sauce and serve garnished with parsley.

TOMATO AND CHICKEN BALTI

This is a superb dish, rich with the flavours of tomato and aromatic spices. Serve it with a lentil dish and plain boiled rice for a filling main course.

Serves 4

60ml/4 tbsp corn oil

6 curry leaves

2.5ml/½ tsp mixed onion and
  mustard seeds

8 tomatoes, sliced

5ml/1 tsp ground coriander

5ml/1 tsp chilli powder

5ml/1 tsp ground cumin

5ml/1 tsp garlic purée

5ml/1 tsp salt

675g/1½ lb boned and skinned
  chicken, cubed

15ml/1 tbsp sesame seeds, roasted
  (optional)

COOK'S TIP

*To roast sesame seeds, place
15–30ml/1–2 tbsp oil in a
frying pan and fry for
1 minute, shaking the pan to
prevent the seeds burning.*

Heat the corn oil in a balti pan or wok. Add the curry leaves and onion and mustard seeds and cook for about 30–60 seconds. Reduce the heat and add the tomatoes, stirring to mix.

Mix together the coriander, chilli, cumin, garlic purée and salt in a bowl and add to the tomatoes. Stir briefly and then add the cubed chicken and stir-fry for 5–6 minutes until the chicken is lightly browned.

Add 150ml/¼ pint/⅔ cup water and continue cooking, stirring occasionally, until the sauce thickens and the chicken is cooked through. Sprinkle with roasted sesame seeds, if you wish, and serve.

PAN-FRIED TOMATOES WITH TUNA

Add tuna to this combination of tomatoes, black olives and anchovies for a classic Mediterranean meal.

Serves 2

90ml/6 tbsp olive oil

30ml/2 tbsp lemon juice

2 garlic cloves, chopped

5ml/1 tsp chopped fresh thyme

*4 canned anchovy fillets, drained
    and finely chopped*

2 tuna steaks, about 175g/6oz each

225g/8oz plum tomatoes, halved

30ml/2 tbsp chopped fresh parsley

4–6 black olives, pitted and chopped

freshly ground black pepper

crusty bread, to serve

COOK'S TIP

*If tuna steaks are not available,
swordfish steaks make a good
substitute. Alternatively use
salmon fillets. Cook them for a
little longer, about 5–6 minutes
each side.*

Blend together 60ml/4 tbsp of the oil with the lemon juice, garlic, thyme, anchovies and black pepper and pour over the tuna steaks in a shallow non-metallic bowl. Leave to marinate for at least 1 hour.

Preheat the grill. Place the tuna on a grill rack and grill for about 4 minutes each side until the fish feels firm to the touch, basting occasionally with the marinade. Take care not to overcook.

Meanwhile heat the remaining oil in a frying pan and add the tomatoes. Fry for about 2 minutes each side and arrange on two warmed serving plates. Scatter with parsley and olives and top with a tuna steak. Add the remaining marinade to the pan juices and warm through. Pour over the tuna and tomatoes and serve at once with crusty bread.

PRAWN CREOLE

Tomatoes are an important feature in Creole cooking, giving colour, flavour and the necessary sweet acidity for which this cuisine is famous.

Serves 6–8

75g/3oz/6 tbsp unsalted butter

1 large onion, thinly sliced

1 large green pepper, seeded and
    thinly sliced

2 celery sticks, thinly sliced

2 garlic cloves, thinly sliced

1 bay leaf

30ml/2 tbsp paprika

450g/1lb tomatoes, peeled, seeded
    and chopped

250ml/8fl oz/1 cup tomato juice

20ml/4 tsp Worcestershire sauce

4–6 dashes hot pepper sauce

7.5ml/1½ tsp cornflour

1.5kg/3–3½ lb raw prawns, peeled
    and deveined

salt

boiled rice with parsley, to serve

Melt 25g/1oz/2 tbsp of the butter in a large frying pan and fry the onion, pepper, celery, garlic and bay leaf very briefly for 1–2 minutes until hot and coated in butter. Add the paprika, tomatoes, tomato juice and the Worcestershire and hot pepper sauces and stir well to mix. Bring to the boil and simmer, uncovered, for 8–10 minutes until the liquid is reduced by about a quarter and the vegetables have softened. Season with salt.

Blend the cornflour with 75ml/5 tbsp cold water and pour it into the tomato sauce. Stir the sauce continuously over the heat for a couple of minutes until thickened slightly and then remove from the heat.

Melt the remaining butter in a large frying pan and sauté the prawns, in batches if necessary, for 2–4 minutes until pink and tender. When all the prawns are cooked, reheat the tomato sauce and stir in the cooked prawns. Cook for no more than 1 minute. Adjust the seasoning and serve at once with boiled rice.

TOMATO-COATED SWORDFISH

This is a very tasty dish with a rich and satisfying sauce, flavoured with tomatoes, olives, capers and Pecorino cheese that looks and tastes wonderful.

Serves 4

30ml/2 tbsp olive oil

1 small onion, finely chopped

1 celery stick, finely chopped

450g/1lb ripe plum tomatoes, chopped

115g/4oz green olives, pitted, half roughly chopped, half left whole

45ml/3 tbsp drained bottled capers

4 large swordfish steaks, about 1cm/ 1/2in thick and 115g/4oz in weight

1 egg

50g/2oz/2/3 cup grated Pecorino cheese

25g/1oz/1/2 cup fresh white breadcrumbs

salt and freshly ground black pepper

fresh parsley, to garnish

Heat the oil in a large heavy-based frying pan and gently fry the onion and celery for about 3 minutes, stirring frequently. Stir in the tomatoes, olives and capers and season with salt and pepper. Bring to the boil and then reduce the heat, cover and simmer for about 15 minutes, stirring occasionally. Add a little water if the sauce becomes too thick.

Skin the fish and place each steak between two sheets of clear film. Pound lightly with a rolling pin until each steak is about 5mm/1/4in thick. Beat the egg in a bowl and add the cheese, breadcrumbs and a few spoonfuls of the sauce. Stir well to make a moist stuffing. Spread one quarter of the stuffing over each swordfish steak and roll up, securing with a wooden cocktail stick.

Add the rolls to the sauce and bring to the boil. Reduce the heat, cover and simmer gently for about 30 minutes, turning the rolls once. Add a little water as necessary as the sauce reduces.

Remove the rolls from the sauce and discard the cocktail sticks. Place on warmed dinner plates and spoon the sauce over the top. Garnish with parsley and serve immediately.

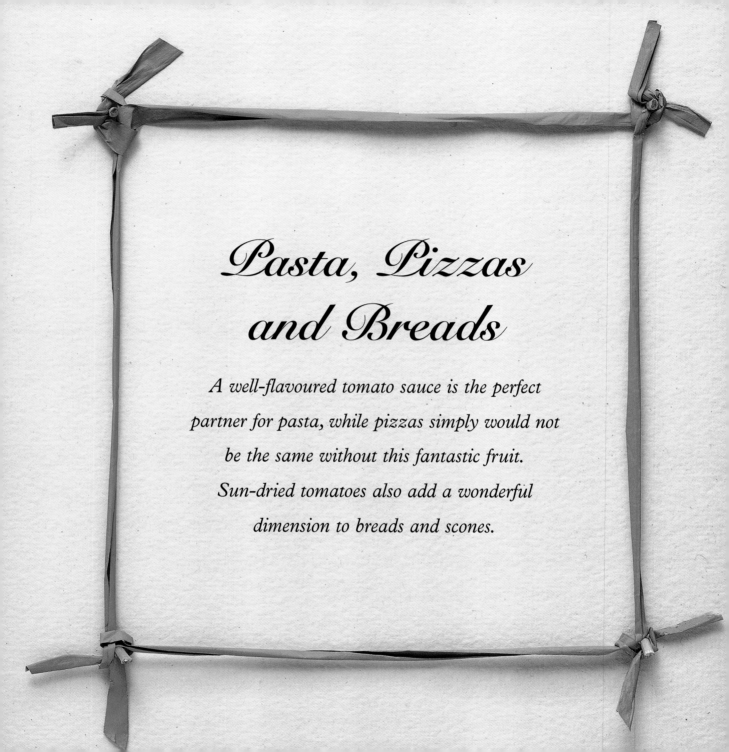

Pasta, Pizzas and Breads

A well-flavoured tomato sauce is the perfect

partner for pasta, while pizzas simply would not

be the same without this fantastic fruit.

Sun-dried tomatoes also add a wonderful

dimension to breads and scones.

TOMATO AND CLAM LINGUINE

You can use fresh or canned tomatoes for this superb dish – both contrast so well with clams.

Serves 4

900g/2lb fresh clams in their shells, scrubbed, or 350g/12oz bottled clams with their liquid

90ml/6 tbsp olive oil

1 garlic clove, crushed

400g/14oz tomatoes, fresh or canned (peeled, cored and seeded if fresh), very finely chopped

350g/12oz linguine

60ml/4tbsp chopped fresh parsley

salt and freshly ground black pepper

Cook the clams in a large pan in a cupful of water, lifting out each clam as soon as it opens. Scoop the clams out of their shells and place in a bowl, reserving any liquid in a separate bowl. Pour the cooking liquid from the pan into the juices from the clams and strain this through kitchen paper to remove any sand. If using bottled clams, use the liquid from the jar.

Heat the olive oil and gently fry the garlic until golden. Discard the garlic and stir in the tomatoes and the clam liquid. Cook gently until the sauce begins to thicken. Cook the pasta according to the instructions on the packet.

A minute or two before the pasta is ready, stir the parsley and clams into the tomato sauce, raise the heat and season. Drain the pasta and place in a serving bowl. Pour on the hot sauce and mix well before serving.

COOK'S TIP

Discard any clams that do not open after cooking. If the clams are large, cut into 2 or 3 pieces.

CANNELLONI AL FORNO

In this classic Italian dish, the filled pasta tubes are cooked in the ever-popular Napoletana Sauce.

Serves 4–6

450g/1lb boned and skinned chicken
  breast, cooked
225g/8oz mushrooms
2 garlic cloves, crushed
30ml/2 tbsp chopped fresh parsley
15ml/1 tbsp chopped fresh tarragon
1 egg, beaten
lemon juice, to taste
12–18 cannelloni tubes
50g/2oz/⅔ cup Parmesan cheese,
  grated
salt and freshly ground black pepper
1 fresh parsley sprig, to garnish

For the Napoletana sauce

900g/2lb ripe tomatoes, chopped
1 onion, chopped
1 carrot, diced
1 celery stick, diced
150ml/¼ pint/⅔ cup dry white
  wine (optional)
1 fresh parsley sprig
pinch of caster sugar
15ml/1 tbsp chopped fresh oregano

Make the Napoletana sauce. Place the tomatoes, onion, carrot, celery, wine, if using, parsley, sugar and seasoning in a saucepan, bring to the boil and simmer, half-covered for 45 minutes until very thick, stirring occasionally. Pour into a blender or food processor and blend until smooth. Strain to remove the tomato seeds and skin, then add the oregano and adjust the seasoning.

Preheat the oven to 200°C/400°F/Gas 6 and butter a large shallow ovenproof dish. Place the chicken in a food processor and blend until finely minced. Transfer to a bowl. Blend the mushrooms, garlic, chopped parsley and tarragon in the food processor and stir into the chicken with the egg, a little lemon juice to taste and plenty of seasoning.

Cook the cannelloni in boiling salted water, according to the instructions on the packet. Drain well on a clean tea towel. Place the filling in a piping bag fitted with a large plain nozzle and fill each tube of cannelloni. Lay the tubes in the prepared dish in a single layer. Pour over the sauce and sprinkle with Parmesan cheese. Bake in the oven for 30–35 minutes until brown and bubbling. Serve garnished with a sprig of parsley.

TOMATO AND MOZZARELLA PIZZA

It may be the simplest, but this great pizza with its tomato and cheese topping is still one of the best.

Serves 2–3

1 commercially prepared pizza base,
*   about 25–30cm/10–12in diameter*
30ml/2 tbsp olive oil
150g/5oz mozzarella cheese,
*   thinly sliced*
2 ripe tomatoes, thinly sliced
6–8 basil leaves
30ml/2 tbsp freshly grated Parmesan
*   cheese*
salt and freshly ground black pepper

For the Italian tomato sauce

15ml/1 tbsp olive oil
1 onion, finely chopped
1 garlic clove, crushed
400g/14oz can chopped tomatoes
15ml/1 tbsp tomato purée
15ml/1 tbsp chopped fresh mixed
*   herbs, such as parsley, thyme, basil*
*   and oregano*
pinch of sugar

Make the tomato sauce. Heat the oil in a pan and fry the onion and garlic for 5 minutes until softened. Add the tomatoes, tomato purée, fresh herbs, sugar and seasoning and simmer, uncovered, for 15–20 minutes until the tomatoes have reduced to a thick pulp.

Preheat the oven to 220°C/425°F/Gas 7. Brush the pizza base with 15ml/1 tbsp of the oil and then spread over the tomato sauce. Arrange the mozzarella and tomato slices, overlapping, on top.

Roughly tear the basil leaves and scatter over the pizza with the grated Parmesan cheese. Drizzle over the remaining oil and season well with black pepper. Bake for 15–20 minutes until crisp and golden. Serve at once.

BARBECUED TOMATO PIZZETTES

If you're barbecuing outdoors, why not try these unusual pizzettes, made with yellow cherry tomatoes.

Serves 6

225g/8oz/2 cups strong white flour
10g/¼ oz sachet easy-blend
   dried yeast
60ml/4 tbsp olive oil
salt

For the topping

1 ripe mango, peeled, stoned and
   diced
150g/5oz wafer-thin sliced smoked
   ham, roughly chopped
150g/5oz Brie, diced
12 yellow cherry tomatoes, halved
salt and freshly ground black pepper

Mix together the flour, yeast and a pinch of salt. Make a well in the centre and stir in 150ml/¼ pint/⅔ cup warm water and 45ml/3 tbsp of the oil. Mix until blended and then knead to make a firm dough. Turn out on to a floured surface and knead for about 5 minutes until smooth. Place in a lightly oiled bowl, cover with oiled clear film and leave in a warm place for 30–40 minutes until the dough is doubled in size and springy to the touch.

Divide the dough into six and roll each piece into a ball. Using your knuckles, press each dough ball into a round about 15cm/6in in diameter, with a raised lip around the edge. Divide the mango, ham and cheese among the pizza bases. Add the tomato halves and sprinkle with salt and pepper. Drizzle the remaining oil over the pizzettes and cook on a medium-hot barbecue for 8–10 minutes until golden brown and crisp underneath.

SUN-DRIED TOMATO BREAD

Sun-dried tomatoes have a wonderful flavour and, used in recipes, give an intense and evocative taste of summer. This bread will remind you of the best of a Tuscan holiday.

Makes 4 small loaves

675g/1½ lb/6 cups strong plain flour

10ml/2 tsp salt

25g/1oz/2 tbsp caster sugar

25g/1oz fresh yeast

*400–475ml/14–16fl oz/1⅔–2 cups
  warm milk*

15ml/1 tbsp tomato purée

*75ml/5 tbsp oil from the jar of sun-
  dried tomatoes*

75ml/5 tbsp olive oil

*75g/3oz/¾ cup drained sun-dried
  tomatoes in oil, chopped*

1 large onion, chopped

Sift the flour, salt and sugar into a bowl and make a well in the centre. Crumble the yeast into 150ml/¼ pint/⅔ cup of the warm milk and add to the flour. Blend the tomato purée with the remaining milk and add to the flour with the tomato oil and olive oil. Mix together to make a dough and then turn out on to a floured surface and knead for about 10 minutes until smooth and elastic. Return to a clean bowl, cover with oiled clear film and leave to rise in a warm place for about 2 hours.

Knock the dough back and add the tomatoes and onion. Knead these into the dough until evenly distributed. Break the dough into four equal pieces and shape into four rounds. Place on a greased baking sheet and cover with a tea towel. Leave to rise again for about 45 minutes.

Preheat the oven to 190°C/375°F/Gas 5. Bake the bread for 40–50 minutes until the loaves sound hollow when tapped underneath. Leave to cool on a wire rack before serving.

COOK'S TIP
A handy trick is to use a pair of sharp kitchen scissors for cutting up sun-dried tomatoes.

TOMATO AND HAM SCONES

The exquisite flavour of sun-dried tomatoes and basil perfectly complements the strong flavour of the ham.

Makes 12

225g/8oz/2 cups self-raising flour

5ml/1 tsp dry mustard

*5ml/1 tsp paprika, plus extra
   for sprinkling*

2.5ml/¹/₂ tsp salt

25g/1oz/2 tbsp butter, softened

15ml/1 tbsp chopped fresh basil

*50g/2oz/¹/₂ cup drained sun-dried
   tomatoes in oil, chopped*

50g/2oz Black Forest ham, chopped

*90–120ml/3–4 fl oz/¹/₃–¹/₂ cup
   semi-skimmed milk, plus extra
   for brushing*

Preheat the oven to 200°C/400°F/Gas 6 and dust a large baking sheet with flour. Sift the flour, mustard, paprika and salt into a bowl and rub in the butter until the mixture resembles breadcrumbs. Stir in the basil, sun-dried tomatoes and ham and mix lightly. Pour in enough milk to mix to a soft dough.

Turn the dough out on to a lightly floured surface, knead lightly and roll out to a 15 x 20cm/6 x 8in rectangle. Cut into 5cm/2in squares and place on the baking sheet. Brush lightly with milk and sprinkle with paprika. Bake in the oven for 12–15 minutes until golden. Transfer to a wire rack to cool.

COOK'S TIP

*Black Forest ham is a robust,
well-flavoured German ham.
Alternatively, you could use
Parma ham or a French
country ham.*

TOMATO BREADSTICKS

Once you've tried this simple recipe, you'll never buy supermarket breadsticks again.

Makes 16

225g/8oz/2 cups plain flour

2.5ml/1/2 tsp salt

7.5ml/1/2 tbsp easy-blend dried yeast

5ml/1 tsp honey

5ml/1 tsp olive oil

6 halves sun-dried tomatoes in oil,
  drained and chopped

15ml/1 tbsp skimmed milk

10ml/2 tsp poppy seeds

Place the flour, salt and yeast in a food processor with the honey and olive oil. Process briefly to mix and then, with the machine running, gradually pour in about 150ml/1/4 pint/2/3 cup warm water to make a soft dough. Process for a further minute more.

Take out the dough and knead for 3–4 minutes on a floured surface until springy and smooth, then knead in the chopped sun-dried tomatoes. Place in a lightly oiled bowl and leave to rise for 5 minutes.

Preheat the oven to 150°C/300°F/Gas 2. Divide the dough into 16 pieces and roll each one into a stick 28cm/11in long and 1cm/1/2in thick. Leave to rise on an oiled baking sheet in a warm place for 15 minutes. Brush the sticks with milk and sprinkle with poppy seeds. Bake for 30 minutes until golden.

Salsas, Relishes and Chutneys

Country people have long known the value of tomatoes in chutneys and relishes. Whether spiced up for salsas or pickled for a rustic-style relish, tomatoes bring a taste of summer just when you need it.

BLOODY MARY RELISH

This is a wonderfully piquant salsa, combining tomatoes, garlic, onions and a dash of vodka and Worcestershire sauce. Serve with fresh oysters for special occasions.

Serves 2

4 ripe tomatoes

1 celery stick

1 garlic clove

2 spring onions

45ml/3 tbsp tomato juice

Worcestershire sauce, to taste

hot pepper sauce, to taste

10ml/2 tsp horseradish sauce

15ml/1 tbsp vodka

juice of 1 lemon

salt and freshly ground black pepper

fresh oysters and wedges of lemon,
    to serve

COOK'S TIP

For a smoother relish, peel, quarter and seed the tomatoes before blending.

Halve the tomatoes and roughly chop the celery. Place with the garlic and spring onions in a food processor or blender and blend until very finely chopped. Transfer to a bowl.

Stir in the tomato juice and add a few drops of Worcestershire sauce and hot pepper sauce to taste. Add the horseradish sauce, vodka and lemon juice and season with salt and pepper. Stir briefly to mix, and serve with oysters and wedges of lemon.

TOMATO AND BACON SALSA

This distinctive tomato salsa is sharpened with lime juice and fresh coriander. The smoky bacon adds an extra dimension to the flavour and, with soured cream, it makes a delicious filling for baked potatoes.

Serves 4

450g/1lb tomatoes

15ml/1 tbsp sunflower oil

4 smoked streaky bacon rashers, finely chopped

45ml/3 tbsp chopped fresh coriander leaves

1 garlic clove, finely chopped

juice of 1 lime

salt and freshly ground black pepper

baked potatoes topped with butter or soured cream, to serve

Peel the tomatoes by plunging them into boiling water for 30 seconds. Refresh in cold water and then peel away the skins. Cut into quarters and remove the cores and seeds. Finely chop the flesh and place in a bowl.

Heat the oil in a frying pan and fry the bacon pieces for 5 minutes until crisp and golden, stirring occasionally. Allow to cool and then mix with the tomatoes. Add the coriander, garlic and lime juice and season with salt and pepper. Transfer to a serving bowl and chill. Serve with baked potatoes topped with butter or soured cream.

COOK'S TIP

For an extra kick, add a dash of hot pepper sauce or a pinch of dried chillies to the salsa.

SWEET POTATOES AND TOMATO SALSA

A tangy tomato and citrus salsa, attractively served in colourful radicchio-leaf cups, provides a wonderful contrast to lightly spiced, succulent sweet potatoes.

Serves 4

500g/1¼ lb sweet potatoes, diced

45ml/3 tbsp olive oil

5ml/1 tsp mustard seeds

5ml/1 tsp cumin seeds

1.5ml/¼ tsp fennel seeds

30ml/2 tbsp dry sherry

4 small radicchio leaves

salt and freshly ground black pepper

fresh basil sprigs, to garnish

For the salsa

2 oranges

1–2 tomatoes

1 spring onion

handful of fresh basil leaves

30ml/2 tbsp olive oil

pinch of sugar

Make the salsa. Peel the oranges with a sharp knife, cut into segments and chop finely. Peel, seed and chop the tomatoes. Slice the spring onion and shred the basil leaves. Mix the salsa ingredients with the oil and sugar in a bowl and season well with salt and pepper. Chill until ready to use.

Cook the sweet potatoes in lightly salted water for 6 minutes. Drain and set aside. Heat the oil in a large frying pan. Add the mustard, cumin and fennel seeds and fry for about 10 seconds until they pop. Stir in the sherry. Add the sweet potatoes, turning to coat them thoroughly, and fry for 10–15 minutes until tender, stirring frequently. Season to taste. Spoon the salsa on to the radicchio leaves and serve with the sweet potatoes. Garnish with basil.

CHUNKY CHERRY TOMATO SALSA

Succulent cherry tomatoes and refreshing cucumber form the base of this delicious, dill-seasoned salsa.

Serves 4

1 cucumber
5ml/1 tsp sea salt
500g/1¼lb cherry tomatoes
juice and grated rind of 1 lemon
45ml/3 tbsp chilli oil
2.5ml/½ tsp dried chilli flakes
1 garlic clove, finely chopped
30ml/2 tbsp chopped fresh dill
salt and freshly ground black pepper

Trim the ends from the cucumber, cut into 2.5cm/1in lengths and then cut each piece lengthways into thin slices. Place in a colander and sprinkle with sea salt. Set aside for 5 minutes until the cucumber has wilted. Wash the cucumber well under cold water and pat dry with kitchen paper.

Quarter the cherry tomatoes and place in a bowl with the cucumber. Place the lemon rind and juice, chilli oil, chilli flakes, garlic and dill in a small jug. Season with salt and pepper and whisk with a fork. Pour the chilli oil dressing over the tomato and cucumber and toss well. Leave to marinate at room temperature for at least 2 hours before serving.

COOK'S TIP
*Try flavouring this salsa
with other fragrant herbs, such
as fresh tarragon, coriander or
even mint.*

TOMATO AND DOUBLE CHILLI SALSA

This is a scorchingly hot salsa for only the brave! Spread it sparingly on to cooked meats and burgers.

Serves 4

6 habanero chillies or Scotch bonnets

2 ripe tomatoes

4 standard green jalapeño chillies

30ml/2 tbsp chopped fresh parsley

30ml/2 tbsp olive oil

15ml/1 tbsp balsamic or
*   sherry vinegar*

salt

Cook's tip

Habanero chillies, or Scotch bonnets, are among the hottest fresh chillies available. You may prefer to tone down the heat of this salsa by using a milder variety of chilli.

Skewer a habanero or Scotch bonnet chilli on a metal fork and hold it in a gas flame for 2–3 minutes, turning the chilli until the skin blackens and blisters. Repeat with all the chillies, then set aside.

Skewer the tomatoes one at a time and hold in the flame for 1–2 minutes, until the skin splits and wrinkles. Slip off the skins, halve the tomatoes, then use a teaspoon to scoop out and discard the seeds. Chop the flesh very finely. Use a clean tea towel to rub the skins off the chillies.

Try not to touch the chillies with your bare hands: use a fork to hold them and slice them open with a sharp knife. Scrape out and discard the seeds, then finely chop the flesh.

Halve the jalapeño chillies, remove their seeds and finely slice them widthways into tiny strips. Mix together both types of chilli, the tomatoes and chopped parsley. Mix the olive oil, vinegar and a little salt, pour this over the salsa and cover the dish. Chill for up to 3 days.

GREEN TOMATO CHUTNEY

Unripened tomatoes are a culinary success rather than a horticultural failure when transformed into this tasty chutney, a perfect accompaniment to strong cheeses and cold cooked meats.

Makes about 2.5kg/5½ lb

1.75kg/4–4½ lb green tomatoes, roughly chopped

450g/1lb apples, peeled, cored and chopped

450g/1lb onions, chopped

2 large garlic cloves, crushed

15ml/1 tbsp salt

45ml/3 tbsp pickling spice

600ml/1 pint/2½ cups cider vinegar

450g/1lb/2 cups granulated sugar

COOK'S TIP

Use a jam funnel to transfer the chutney into the jars. Wipe the jars and label them when cold.

Put the tomatoes, apples, onions and garlic into a large saucepan and add the salt. Tie the pickling spice in a piece of muslin and add to the pan. Pour in the vinegar and add the sugar. Bring to the boil and then reduce the heat and simmer, uncovered, for 1–1½ hours or until the chutney is thick, stirring frequently.

Remove the muslin bag from the chutney. Spoon the hot chutney into warm sterilized jars, cover with airtight, vinegar-proof lids and store for at least 1 month before using.

CACHUMBAR

Cachumbar is a salad relish most commonly served with Indian curries. There are many versions, although this one, with tomatoes and coriander, will leave your mouth feeling cool and fresh.

Serves 4

3 ripe tomatoes

2 spring onions, chopped

1.5ml/¼ tsp caster sugar

45ml/3 tbsp chopped fresh coriander

pinch of salt

1 fresh coriander sprig, to garnish

Core and seed the tomatoes and chop the flesh finely. Mix with the spring onions, sugar, chopped coriander and salt in a bowl. Leave for about 1 hour to allow the flavours to mingle, stir again and serve at room temperature, garnished with a sprig of coriander.

COOK'S TIP
Cachumbar also makes a good accompaniment to fresh crab, lobster or shellfish.

INDEX